LOOK INSIDE

A VICTORIAN SCHOOLROOM

BRIAN MOSES
Illustrated by Adam Hook

WAYLAND

Editor: Jason Hook
Designer: Ian Winton

This edition published in 1999 by Wayland Publishers Ltd
Find Wayland on the Internet at http://www.wayland.co.uk

First published in 1997 by Wayland Publishers Ltd,
61 Western Road, Hove, East Sussex BN3 1JD, England

© Copyright 1997 Wayland Publishers Ltd

British Library Cataloguing in Publication Data
Moses, Brian, 1950
  Look inside a Victorian schoolroom
  1. Classrooms - England - History - 19th century
  Juvenile literature
  I. Title II. A Victorian schoolroom
  372.9'42
ISBN 0 7502 2555 6

Printed and bound by G.Canale & CSpA, Turin, Italy
Colour reproduction by Page Turn, Hove, England

Cover pictures: A Victorian object lesson (centre);
a school bell (bottom left); a slate and pencil (top right); an
abacus (bottom right).

Picture acknowledgements: All pictures are from Beamish,
The North of England Open Air Museum, except: Mary
Evans 4 (centre), 9 (bottom), 18 (bottom), 22 (top); Fine
Art Photographs 23; Hulton Getty Collection 12 (left), 14
(centre), 20 (right), 22 (bottom-right), 26 (bottom), 28
(bottom), 29 (centre); Billie Love Collection 6 (top), 8
(top), 11 (top), 21 (top), 24 (centre, bottom), 25 (top);
NHPA 29 (bottom); Norfolk Museums Service 11 (bottom),
13 (bottom), 16 (bottom); Popperfoto 6 (bottom), 8
(centre), 10 (bottom); Topham 15 (centre).

All quotes are credited on page 31.

CONTENTS

SCHOOLROOM

TAKING YOUR SEAT

Look inside a Victorian schoolroom. Row upon row of children are sitting in a tall, stuffy room, gloomily lit by gaslights. Their desks rise in tiers or 'galleries' so that the teacher can see right to the back of the class. One girl sits on her hands to make her hard, wooden bench a little bit more comfortable.

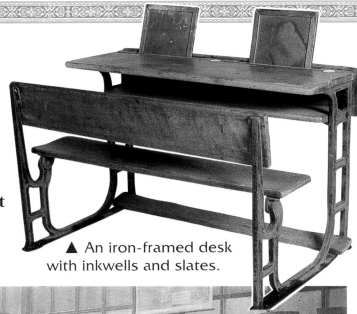

▲ An iron-framed desk with inkwells and slates.

▲ A schoolroom in 1900 with desks rising in tiers.

The walls of a Victorian schoolroom were quite bare, except perhaps for an embroidered text. On the walls of one infant school was the grim warning: 'All liars shall have their part in the lake that burneth with fire and brimstone.'

◄ A pupil embroidered this text in 1853.

Curtains were used to divide the schoolhouse into classrooms. The shouts of several classes competed as they were taught side by side. There was little fresh air because the windows were built high in the walls, to stop pupils looking outside and being distracted from their work.

A VICTORIAN POETRY BOOK

Here we are back again! Lots of work and lots of pain!

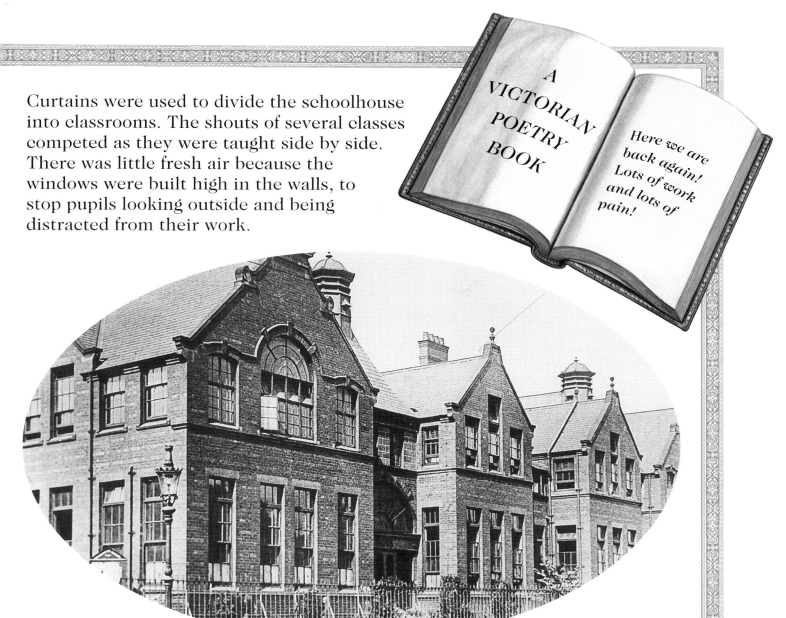

▲ This school was built in the 1870s.

'No painting has been done for above eleven years, indeed the woodwork is decaying for the want of it. A considerable sum needs spending on decoration and on the furniture, particularly the desks which are old and rickety, making it almost impossible to teach a fair hand.' [1]

Many schools were built in the Victorian era, between 1837 and 1901. In the country you would see barns being converted into schoolrooms. Increasing numbers of children began to attend, and the schoolrooms became more and more crowded. But because school managers didn't like to spend money on repairs, buildings were allowed to rot and broken equipment was not replaced.

TEACHERS

A DANGEROUS JOB

A young teacher faces the class, tapping the board loudly with a piece of chalk. He tells the pupils to pick up their slates and draw the objects he has placed in the centre of the room. Two older teachers peer over the children's shoulders.

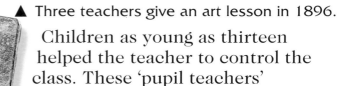
▲ Three teachers give an art lesson in 1896.

Children as young as thirteen helped the teacher to control the class. These 'pupil teachers' scribbled notes for their lessons in books like this one. They received certificates like the one shown here, which helped them qualify as teachers when they were older.

▲ A pupil teacher's notebook and certificate from 1876.

In schools before 1850, you might see a single teacher instructing a class of over 100 children with the help of pupils called 'monitors'. The head teacher quickly taught these monitors, some of them as young as nine, who then tried to teach their schoolmates.

◀ Pupils and teachers in a school photograph from 1890.

Salaries were low, and there were more women teaching than men. The pale, lined faces of older teachers told a story. Some taught only because they were too ill to do other jobs. The poor conditions in schools simply made their health even worse.

Elder sisters,
you may work,
Work and help
your mothers,

Darn the
stockings,
Mend the shirts,
Father's things,
and brother's.

Annual Salaries: Anglebury Elementary School, Dorset, 1863.

Thomas Courtney, Certified Master, £50 per annum plus house, coal and candles.

Peter Hayter, Assistant Master, £18.15s per annum plus free lodging with the Master.

Edith Godwin, Temporary Infants Mistress, £12.10s per annum.

John Farley, Pupil Teacher, £10.5s per annum.

Muriel Grant, Pupil Teacher, £4.10s per annum.

▲ Teachers from Hamsterley School, Durham, photographed before 1900.

◄ A teacher learns to box.

Sometimes, teachers were attacked by angry parents. They shouted that their children should be at work earning money, not wasting time at school. Teachers in rough areas had to learn to box! One wrote in 1886: 'A boy having been punished, I received a note from his mother saying that she would take the nose out of my face.'

'Teachers are expected to perform miracles ... Throughout the year I have felt underneath my work. I have sought change of air, medical advice ... but my doctor tells me nothing will do me good but complete rest. Query. How can a teacher obtain rest?' [2]

PUPILS

BAREFOOT AND RAGGED

Not one of the children is wearing any sort of school uniform. One group of lads look like they are dressed in old rags. Their faces are covered in grime and muck, and some wear nothing on their filthy feet.

▲ Only some of the pupils wear boots in this 1894 group.

'One or two are tidy-looking boys; one has a clean, washed face and a white collar on. The rest are ragged, ill-kempt and squalid in appearance. Some are filthy dirty, others sickly looking with sore eyes ... In the girls' department it is the same ... Children are pointed out to us stunted in growth, with faces old beyond their years.' 3

▲ A ragged child in London.

After 1870, all children from five to thirteen had to attend school by law. In winter in the countryside, many children faced a teeth-chattering walk to school of several miles. A large number didn't turn up.

'Some of them carried two hot potatoes, which had been in the oven, or in the ashes all night, to warm their hands on the way, and to serve as a light lunch on arrival.' 4

◄ A schoolchild with hot-potato hand warmers!

Lessons lasted from 9 am to 5 pm, with a two-hour lunch break. Because classes were so large, pupils all had to do the same thing at the same time. The teacher barked a command, and the children all opened their books. At a second command they began copying sentences from the blackboard.

◀ Not all Victorian school-children could afford boots like these.

'One thing at a time And that done well,

Is a very good rule, As many can tell.

'When you return to school on Monday morning let's have you turn up early with your boots cleaned and a nice clean collar ... remember, a nice clean neck and no high watermark (meaning wash your neck properly, not just down to your collar).' [5]

When pupils found their work boring, teachers found their pupils difficult to control. One unhappy teacher in Victorian London called the children he taught: 'Dirty, foul-mouthed blackguards ... who came not from homes, but from lairs.'

▼ Pupils wore their best clothes for this 1893 school photograph.

REGISTER

▶ The cover and inside (below) of a school register printed in 1889.

MAKING EXCUSES

To start the day, the teacher calls out the pupils' names and ticks all those present in a large register. There are many absences. One girl says that her little brother is away working in the wheat fields, scaring birds with a rattle, and she must take him his lunch at two o'clock!

A look inside the diaries or 'logbooks' kept by Victorian teachers shows that children made excuses for missing school which would not be accepted today: 'I had chilblains and couldn't get my boots on' ... 'I went hop-picking' ... 'There was a wild beasts show in town'.

◀ A blackboard for marking attendance.

▲ Some children earned money picking hops instead of going to school.

Farmers and factory owners employed school-children as cheap labour. One Devon teacher complained: 'Sent to one farmer for six boys employed in mangel picking. Received a message to the effect that when he wanted boys he would have them.'

My head doth ache, My hand doth shake, I have a naughty pen,

My ink is bad, My pen is worse, How can I write well then?

◀ This country school in 1890 is heated by a stove.

Some children worked from 5 am planting potatoes, gathering stones or hay-making, then went to school. After school, they went back to work until 10 pm. When you are yawning during a lesson, just imagine how tired they felt. Fumes from the smelly stoves which heated the schoolroom in winter made the pupils even more sleepy.

▲ A coal stove from a Victorian schoolroom.

▶ Some schools offered medals for good attendance.

Gradually, parents began to take pride in their children's learning and made sure that their names were ticked off in the register every day.

'September 24th 1883: Two boys, George Flisher and George Falkner, having made the full 400 attendances had their school fees for the year refunded and placed in a savings bank. Louisa Spillet was also treated in like manner for making most attendances (397) among the girls.' [6]

BLACKBOARD

CHALK AND TALK

The teacher wheels a blackboard to the front of the class. With a squealing of chalk, he writes up a series of sums, reading them out as he goes. One boy lets out a loud yawn. At a word of command, every pupil picks up his slate and begins to copy down the sums from the board.

▲ A 'chalk and talk' maths lesson in Edinburgh, 1850.

Procrastination is the thief of Time.

Dr. Edward Young.

▲ A Victorian blackboard.

Victorian lessons concentrated on the 'three Rs' - Reading, wRiting and aRithmetic. Children learnt by reciting things like parrots, until they were word perfect. It was not an exciting form of learning!

Teachers taught with 'chalk and talk'. The teacher chalked some words or sums on the blackboard and talked about them. The children then copied what was written there. You might see a history lesson written on the blackboard like this:

Q. Who was Henry VIII?
A. Son of Henry VII.

Q. What was his character?
A. As a young man he was bluff, generous, right royal and very handsome.

Q. How was he when he grew older?
A. He was bloated, vain, cruel and selfish.

Science was taught through an 'object lesson'. Snails, models of trees (like those in the picture), sunflowers, stuffed dogs, crystals, wheat or pictures of elephants and camels were placed on each pupil's desk as the subject for the lesson.

We march to our places,
With clean hands and faces,
And pay great attention to all we are told.

For we know we shall never Be happy and clever; But learning is better than silver and gold.

▲ An object lesson, studying trees.

► A Victorian globe.

▼ How does this timetable from 1872 compare to your own?

The object lesson was supposed to make children observe, then talk about what they had seen. Unfortunately, many teachers found it easier to chalk up lists describing the object, for the class to copy. Geography involved yet more copying and reciting - listing the countries shown on a globe, or chanting the names of railway stations between London and Holyhead.

Look at a timetable from late in the 1800s and you will see a greater number of subjects, including needlework, cookery and woodwork. But the teacher still taught them by chalking and talking.

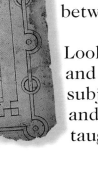

SLATES AND COPYBOOKS

LEARNING YOUR LETTERS

A group of young children sit glumly in one corner. They each have a wooden tray full of sand on their desk. The children practise writing the letter 'A' by drawing in the sand with their fingers. Then they smooth out the sand and copy the next letter from the blackboard. One girl rests her head on her neighbour's shoulder and falls fast asleep.

▲ A sand-tray.

◀ Too young to write on slates, these infants use sand-trays to learn their letters.

Children learnt to write on slates, like the one shown here. They scratched letters on them with sharpened pieces of slate. Paper was expensive, but slates could be used again and again. Children were supposed to bring sponges to clean them. Most just spat on the slates, and rubbed them clean with their sleeves.

◀ Sums scratched on a slate.

*'I wrote endlessly in copybooks -
"A stitch in time saves nine",
"Too many cooks spoil the broth" -
but I never composed, much less wrote in class, a
single original sentence.'* [7]

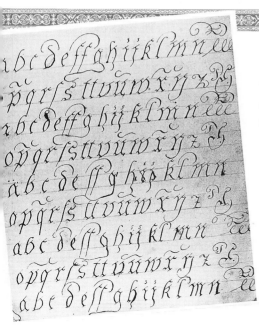

◀ This 'copperplate' copybook was used in 1842.

While hewing yews,
Hugh lost his ewe
And put it in
the hue and cry,
You brought the
ewe back by
and by

And only begged
the hewer's ewe;
Your hands
to wash
in water pure.

Older children learnt to use pen and ink by writing in 'copybooks'. Each morning the ink monitor filled up little, clay inkwells and handed them round from a tray. Pens were fitted with scratchy, leaking nibs, and children were punished for spilling ink which 'blotted their copybooks'.

▼ A class in 1890 practise their writing.

Teachers also gave dictation, reading out strange poems like the one in our Victorian poetry book (above), which the children had to spell out correctly.

▼ This copybook looks more fun than most.

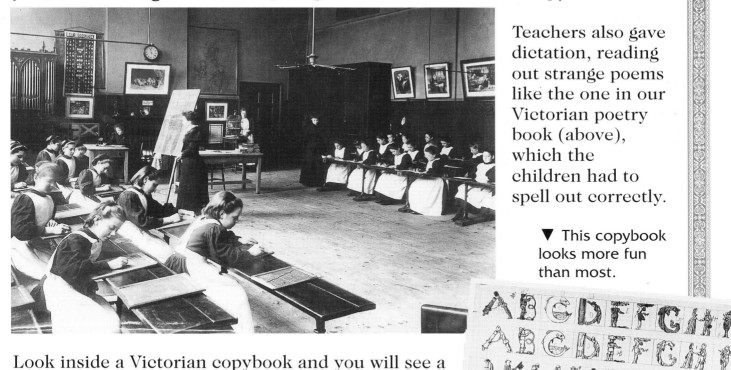

Look inside a Victorian copybook and you will see a spidery writing style called 'copperplate'. Children copied proverbs printed in the copybook, like 'Waste not, want not', on to the blank lines beneath. Victorian teachers wanted everyone to work in the same way, like robots, so left-handed children were forced to use their right hands!

READER

▲ A Victorian Bible.

BIBLES AND STORYBOOKS

Slates showing the pictures and names of different objects hang from the walls of the infants' class. The children chant the name of each object in turn. When they can use these words in sentences they will move on to a 'reader'. This will probably not be a story book, but the Bible.

▲ These children learnt words from the classroom wall.

And see! oh, what a dreadful thing!
The fire has caught her apron-string;
Her apron burns, her arms, her hair —
She burns all over everywhere.

Then how the pussy-cats did mew —
What else, poor pussies, could they do?
They screamed for help, 'twas all in vain!
So then they said 'We'll scream again;
Make haste, make haste, me-ow, me-o,
She'll burn to death, we told her so.'

So she was burnt, with all her clothes,
And arms, and hands, and eyes, and nose;
Till she had nothing more to lose
Except her little scarlet shoes;
And nothing else but these was found
Among her ashes on the ground.

For reading lessons, the pupils lined up with their toes touching a semi-circle chalked on the floor. They took it in turns to read aloud from the Bible. The words didn't sound like everyday words, and children stumbled over the long sentences. Quicker readers fidgeted as they waited for their turn to read.

◀ The story Harriet and the Matches warns children not to play with fire.

School inspectors slowly realized that the Bible's language was too difficult. They thought children might blame religion for their reading problems! Bibles were gradually replaced by books of moral stories, with titles like *Harriet and the Matches*.

You will never be sorry
For using gentle words,
For doing your best,
For being kind to the poor.

For looking before leaping,
For thinking before speaking,
For doing what you can to make others happy.

◄ Few schools could afford a beautiful reader like this one.

A reader had to last for a whole year. If the class read it too quickly, they had to go back to the beginning and read it all over again!

Newer books at least helped a child's imagination to escape the walls of the gloomy schoolroom. One schoolchild wrote: 'I learned of a world beyond. In fancy I got wrecked on Coral Island or shared the adventures of Robinson Crusoe.'

◄ Waiting to read aloud was dull for quicker readers.

ABACUS

THE SCHOOL INSPECTOR

The pupils stare wide-eyed when the white-whiskered school inspector strides into the schoolroom. The class watch as he tests one terrified girl on her maths. The inspector growls questions on the 'four rules' - addition, subtraction, multiplication and division. With trembling hands the girl slides beads along the wires of a calculating machine called an abacus.

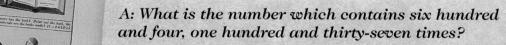

▲ Victorian children used an abacus like this as a calculator.

▲ A girls' science class studying the weather vane on the teacher's desk.

▼ A book of maths problems from 1880.

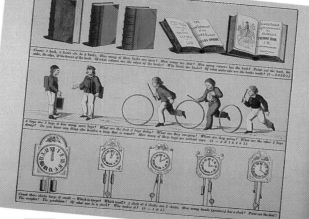

Maths problems on cards were handed out to the class. The following puzzles were given to schoolchildren in 1890. If you had been in school that day, would you have known the answers?

A: *What is the number which contains six hundred and four, one hundred and thirty-seven times?*

B: *Fifty hens laid an egg every other day for 28 days. What profit would be made by selling the eggs at three and a half pence each if the hens each cost a half penny a day for their food?*
(The answers are on page 31)

A set of imperial weights. ◀

Two pints will make one quart, Four quarts one gallon strong,

Some drink too little, Some too much, To drink too much is wrong.

Calculations were made using imperial weights and measures instead of our simpler metric system. The Victorian poem in our book (above) and this sum, set in a Suffolk school in 1890, use imperial measurements:

C: How many furlongs, rods, yards, feet, inches and barleycorns will reach round the earth, supposing it to be 25,020 miles? (See page 31)

◀ The teacher counted time on this 'clicker' as the class recited their tables.

Children had to pass inspections in maths, reading and writing before they could move up to the next class or 'standard'. Teachers were also tested by the dreaded inspector, to make sure that they deserved government funds - just as your teachers are today.

▶ The school inspector tests a girl on her mental arithmetic.

CANE

TAKING YOUR PUNISHMENT

Swishing his cane, the teacher sneaks up behind a daydreamer who is making inkblots in his maths book. Siezing the boy by the belt, the teacher lifts him wriggling into the air, and thrashes him across the backside until he screams for mercy.

◄ The cane was an important part of harsh schoolroom discipline.

'I never remember seeing my headmaster in school when he had not a cane hanging by the crook of his left wrist.' [8]

◄ This leather strap or 'tawse' was used to thrash children.

► Some teachers placed misbehaving pupils in a 'punishment basket' suspended by a rope from the ceiling!

Teachers handed out regular canings. Look inside the 'punishment book' that every school kept, and you will see many reasons for these beatings: rude conduct, leaving the playground without permission, sulkiness, answering back, missing Sunday prayers, throwing ink pellets and being late.

If this book should chance to roam,

Box its ears and send it home.

Punishment Book
'January 25th 1883. Punished Alfred Payne this morning with the cane for playing truant.
January 26th 1883. Punished John King this afternoon with the cane for not telling the truth.' [9]

▼ No wonder this class of 1896 looks so well behaved!

Boys were caned across their bottoms, and girls across their hands or bare legs. Some teachers broke canes with their fury, and kept birch rods in jars of water to make them more supple. Victims had to choose which cane they wished to be beaten with! At one school, boys threw slates at the teacher in revenge for the caning they had received.

Punishment Book
'October 20th 1870: Mrs. D. brought her two sons to be flogged prescribing as an effectual remedy for truant-playing, reading verses of the Scriptures, with a stripe at the conclusion of each, on the back with a stout cane.' [10]

◄ Imagine having to read the Bible while being caned!

DUNCE'S CAP

GO TO THE BACK OF THE CLASS

The boy's punishment does not end with his caning. He is made to stand on a stool at the back of the class, wearing an armband with 'DUNCE' written on it. The teacher then takes a tall, cone-shaped hat decorated with a large 'D', and places it on the boy's head. He had taken his caning without tears, but being labelled a 'dunce' makes him cry and cry.

◀ A cartoon from 1900 of a 'dunce'.

▲ 'D' stands for 'Dunce' on this Victorian dunce's cap.

▲ Victorian children lived in fear of being caned and called a dunce.

Punishment Book
'September 21st 1885: A girl named Alice Lot, who had been playing truant, was this day punished for so doing, by wearing a small slate fastened around her neck with the words "The truant girl".' [11]

Look inside a Victorian schoolroom and you might see pupils wearing badges saying 'truant' or 'dunce'. Teachers believed that children who wore these labels would be embarrassed into trying harder.

'Displayed on hooks upon the wall in all their terrors were the cane and ruler; and near them, on a shelf of its own, the dunce's cap, made of old newspapers and decorated with glaring wafers [letters] of the largest size.' [12]

A boy that is good Will learn his book well,

And if he can't read Will strive for to spell.

Today we know that some children learn more slowly than others. Victorian teachers believed that all children could learn at the same speed, and if some fell behind then they should be punished for not trying hard enough. One girl said of her teachers: 'They thought the only way to manage children were to frighten 'em to death.'

▲ In this Victorian painting, a girl wears a dunce's cap made from old newspapers.

WOODWORK TOOLS

DIFFERENT LESSONS

In the afternoon, while the boys study woodwork, the girls learn cookery. Yesterday, they made rock cakes that were as hard as rocks. Today's lesson is how to cook a cheap Sunday roast. Eighteen girls crowd around one table, helping the teacher to prepare a single lamb chop for the oven!

▼ Learning to cook, in 1899.

Boys and girls took separate lessons to prepare them for when they left school. Girls were not trained for careers as they are today, but for marriage. They were shown how to do housework and cook meals cheaply. They also learnt how to embroider 'samplers', which were moral texts decorated with pictures of small birds, butterflies and flowers.

▶ Girls in 1900 learning to iron collars and cuffs.

24

Look inside a schoolroom in the 1890s and you might see boys practising farming, gardening, shoemaking, technical drawing and various handicrafts. At Beethoven Street School in Paddington, London, older boys learnt woodwork from the school caretaker, who was also a carpenter! These different lessons prepared boys for earning a wage.

SAMPLER POEM

Be gracious to Thy servant, Lord, do Thou my life defend,

That I according to Thy word My future time may spend.

▼ A boys' woodwork lesson in 1897.

▲ Victorian woodwork tools.

DOING DRILL

When it is time for PE or 'drill', a pupil teacher starts playing an out-of-tune piano. The children jog, stretch and lift weights in time to the awful music. It is like a Victorian aerobics class! Even when the teacher rings a heavy, brass bell to announce the end of school, the pupils march out to the playground in perfect time.

'All the children in a class came out together ... to a series of commands. 'One!' and you stood in your desk. 'Two!' and you put your left leg over the seat. 'Three!' and the right joined in. 'Four!' you faced the lane between the classes. 'Five!' you marched on the spot. 'Six!' you stepped forward and the pupil teacher chanted, 'Left, right, left, right'. It was agony, you were so longing to get outside. But if one boy pushed another you would have to go back and begin the rigmarole again.' [13]

▼ Many drill lessons took place in the playground.

▶ A Victorian teacher's bell.

Drill was used both for exercise and to teach obedience. There was not much sports equipment in the school, so children exercised in time to music or lifted dumb-bells. They also had to march around the school like soldiers and follow orders at the blast of the teacher's whistle.

Children who do drill,
Seldom are ill,
Seldom look pale,
Delicate and frail,
Seldom are sulky.

Seldom are spiteful,
But always delightful.
So dears,
I still
Beg you to drill.

◄ This teacher and the girls crouching down are all holding dumb-bells.

◄ A boy performs his winter drill.

▲ Victorian dumb-bells.

'We hated drill, especially when it was cold. In the winter we had to do it with our hats and coats on. The teachers didn't even get to move around, but had to stand at the front shouting instructions so they liked it even less than us.' 14

HOOPS AND CONKERS

IN THE PLAYGROUND

Outside the classroom is a small yard crowded with shrieking schoolmates. Games of blindman's buff, snakes and ladders, hide-and-seek and hopscotch are in full swing. Some boys have begged a pig's bladder from the butcher, which they have blown up to use as a football. Others are drilling hobnails through cotton reels to make spinning tops. The group nearest you crouches over a game of marbles.

▼ This picnic was part of a school outing in 1857.

▲ A game of marbles in 1890.

► A Victorian snakes and ladders board.

In Victorian city schools, playgrounds were surrounded by high brick walls, but one woman remembers her country school as having 'a playground with birch trees and turf, bald in places, the whole being enclosed within pointed, white-painted railings.'

Winter games were just like those you play today. Slides were made on the ice which covered playground puddles, and furious snowball battles were fought.

Girls skipped while singing rhymes, like those in our poetry book, which predicted their futures. Would they marry a rich man, poor man, beggar man or thief?

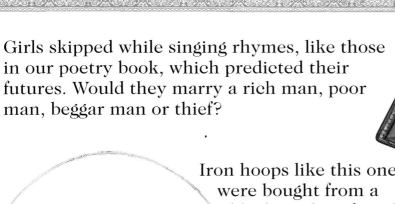

This year, next year; Sometime, never.

Big house, little house, Pigsty, barn.

Tinker, tailor; Soldier, sailor; Rich man, poor man, Beggar man, thief!

Iron hoops like this one were bought from a blacksmith or found on an old barrel. The hoop was then rolled around the playground with a stick. There were no teachers on playground duty, leaving bigger children free to bully smaller ones.

▲ A hoop and stick.

► A hoop race in about 1900.

Different seasons brought different games. When children shook their first conker from the trees, threaded it, and polished it for battle, they chanted:

'Obbly, obbly, onker!
My first conker!
I tilly ack! My first crack!'

◄ Pick the hardest conker for battle!

GLOSSARY

Blackguards (pronounced blaggards) Scoundrels, wicked and dishonest people.

Chilblains Painful swellings, especially on the foot, caused by cold.

Copperplate A style of writing using thin, sloping letters.

Darn Mend a hole by weaving yarn.

Dictation Reading something aloud for children to write down as accurately as they can.

Dunce An insulting name for someone who is slow at learning.

Embroidered Decorated with needlework.

Hobnails Heavy nails used on boot-soles.

Ill-kempt Unkempt, untidy.

Inspection A visit by an inspector to test the school, teachers and pupils.

Logbook A book in which day-to-day details of school life are recorded.

Managers (now often called governors) A group of people who oversee a school.

Per Annum Each year.

Rickety Weak, likely to collapse.

Rigmarole A long, complicated process or procedure.

Slate A grey rock that can be easily split into flat plates for writing on.

Squalid Disgustingly dirty.

Standards The Victorian name for the different school years.

Stunted Not properly or fully developed.

Thrifty Careful with money.

Tiered Arranged in a series of levels.

Truant A child who stays away from school without permission.

FURTHER READING

MEASUREMENTS

Furlong – 201 metres

Rod – 5 metres

Yard – 0.914 metres

Foot – 0.305 metres

Inch – 2.5 centimetres

Barleycorn – 0.8 centimetres

Gallon – 4 litres

Quart – 1.136 litres

Pint – 568 millilitres

MATHS ANSWERS

A: 82,748

B: The profit is 1750 pence. In decimal money, this would be £17.50, but the Victorians used a system of money in which £1 contained 20 shillings, and 1 shilling contained 12 pence. So a Victorian child's answer would be 7 pounds, 5 shillings, 10 pence!

C: 25,020 Miles = 200,160 Furlongs = 8,006,400 Rods = 44,035,200 Yards = 132,105,600 Feet = 1,585,267,200 Inches = 4,755,801,600 Barleycorns.
No wonder they needed an abacus!

QUOTES

The quotes from Victorian teachers and schoolchildren can be found in the following books:

1 *Spare the Rod*, Journal of a Victorian Schoolmaster in Dorset, 1863-4.
2 *The Victorian and Edwardian Schoolchild*, Pamela Horn.
3 *Life and Labour of the London Poor*, Charles Booth.
4 *Lark Rise to Candleford*, Flora Thompson, 1939.
5 *Poverty, Hardship but Happiness*, Albert Paul, quoted in *Ordinary Lives 100 Years Ago*, Carol Adams, 1982.
6 *An Elementary School Logbook*, Longman Secondary History.
7 *The Victorian Schoolroom*, Trevor May, 1995.
8 *A Short History of English Schools,* Christopher Martin, 1979.
9 *An Elementary School Logbook*, Longman Secondary History.
10 St Paul's C of E Combined Schools Logbook, Leamington Spa, in *Finding Out About Victorian Schools*, Amanda Clarke.
11 *An Elementary School Logbook*, Longman Secondary History.
12 *The Old Curiosity Shop*, Charles Dickens, 1841.
13 *Joseph Ashby of Tysoe*, Mabel Ashby, quoted in *Ordinary Lives 100 Years Ago*, Carol Adams, 1982.
14 *School Day*, Monica Stoppleman, 1990.

BOOKS TO READ

Deary, Terry *The Vile Victorians* (Hippo, 1994)

Ferguson, Sheila *Growing Up in Victorian Britain* (Batsford, 1977)

Horn, Pamela *The Victorian and Edwardian Schoolchild* (Alan Sutton, 1989)

Longley, Andrew *Victorian Britain* (Hamlyn, 1994)

Stoppleman, Monica *School Day* (A & C Black, 1990)

Tames, Richard *What Do We Know About Victorian Britain?* (Macdonald Young, 1994)

Triggs, Tony *Victorian Britain* (Wayland, 1990)

Wood, Richard *A Victorian School* (Wayland, 1993)

INDEX